ISBN: 978-0-6151-4458-0

"Mine eyes hath seen…"
Poetry

By Melvin Eddings

Preface

Poetry comes in different forms, times, patterns and most of all passions. For me, my life has been the author of my poetry. The loves, trials, tribulations, and pains leading to joys and vice-versa are what encompass my writings. As life shows up and presents itself... I write. Yes, I write to express my inner most feelings. Most of all, I write what others are afraid to say or feel. However, I write out of love, for love and with love.

Dedication

To my mother Ruby L. Eddings, for handing down all of life's lessons with love. To all the women in my life that taught me to be patient and that healing is a process. To all the men who lived by example and not by denial.

Table of Contents:

"HAPPINESS"

Everyone everywhere is searching for happiness.

Look up into the skies, and the skies become endless.

Our vision, however individually, reaches a certain altitude, and then it stops.

The same as if you are peering from the peak of the highest mountain.

You look to search around you-
Vision, your vision can only peer so far.

As you live and learn, wisdom presents itself.
You realize that innate ability.

Your conclusion finds its resting place.

You realize that all the happiness,
 you've search so long for

Was always right inside of you!

"And I dream..."

Of our love lasting the time to count grains of sand in twenty hourglasses;

While lying in fields of Hyacinths, treasuring each moment that passes.

Of blue green waters clear as crystal, rolling upon white beaches;

You and I are one in breath as a rhythm of drumbeats teaches.

How love can be carried through the air for miles in a song.

And leave romance looming indiscreetly all the night long.

Of being your protector for life, along with your mascot of love;

Sharing a timeless clock, God the timekeeper directly from Heaven above.

Of never living without you, never engaging in a loving yet final touch;

For me you are everything beautiful in life, and that encompasses much.

And I dream of seeing you walk down the aisle, your figure dancing gracefully as you smile, because you know you are captivating.

You've garnered the attention of all; you are the mistress of the ball.

You send one's inquisitiveness escalating.

So this dream finally makes its way through the corridors of reality.

I no longer have to dream your mine, keeping you mine is my formality.

It is your turn to pinch yourself to see if this love is a series of dreams.

Or if it is the best of the best, and everything is just as it seems.

I'll save you the time, you need not guess if this love is real.

It is as real as it gets, all the benefits, features, highlights and thrills, neatly bundled in a once in a life time deal.

You need only to hold on tight and enjoy the ride; only God knows its length.

However, you never need to worry about falling off or out, because it is also God who gives it strength.

"IT'S ALL ABOUT <u>LOVE</u>!"

As the sun shines, it illuminates the worlds display.

Showing off its wonders and glory of perfection in a loving array.

Scattered about in a perfect blend of colors, pastels and hues.

Trees with its green, flowers red, yellow and pink, water with its blues.

Birds chirping with each other in song, while the fish move up stream.

Deer finding new forests to graze, as the bear awakens from a hibernator's dream.

Time is its own consultant, the manager of all things whether it is old or new.

It constantly progress, never stops, and never asks if you are finished or through.

Time was designed with love; it gives you opportunity and chance.

It challenges you to be persistent as your abilities to manage enhance.

Nothing remains the same; everything changes with or in time.

Relationships for better or worst, and seasons stay in rhythm and rhyme.

Love has witnessed the tests of time, only true **LOVE** will prevail.

Simply put "it's all about love" it is the main ingredient life entails.

Can you imagine life without love?

There would be no acts of kindness, no friendly gestures or even a smile.

No heartfelt kisses or no one to reach out and touch for at least a mile.

Birthdays, holidays, anniversaries, there would be nothing to celebrate.

No reason to have good cheer and the world would be filled with hate.

Nature's progressing while being true to itself, acting out seasonable.

While the Creator allows man the will of choice, if man chooses to be reasonable.

Challenge time; use it wisely, for what the Creator designed it for from above.

Waste not another moment remember "it's all about **Love!**"

"Are you the one?"

Are you the one that mesmerize my moments without leaving a clue?

Allowing my dreams to be non-filtered yet shaded in blue.

Are you the one that captivates my thoughts filling them with hope?

Giving me natural desires to chase my passions when others find it hard to cope.

Are you the one that speaks love into my existence allowing me to explore?

The winds of trust, the clouds of joy, and faithfulness at its core.

Are you the one that shines my armor and set my course day to day?

Removing my pitfalls, my stumbling blocks and obstacles along my way.

Are you the one that whispers to me when I try to imply my will?

The same one that said to me "my son, peace be still!"

Are you the one that enlists me to bow down and supplicate?

To remember that you are the "Great I am" and my life I dedicate.

Are you the one that made the footprints in the sand?

The times I felt weak and vulnerable, and pain I couldn't withstand.

Are you the one that nudges me to awaken each and every morn?

The one in the same that has followed me since I was born.

Are you the one?

Are you?

I just wanted to say THANKS!

The Sensation of <u>YOU</u>...

As you reached into the mixture of touch, your sensual radiance found my skin.

My soul explodes with delightful splendor, elevated by grandeur; it's next of kin.

One could only imagine how magnificent you are, in real life, outside of all my dreams.

My life has been filled over and over with rainbows, yet your love has the best color scheme.

Within the boundaries of one last breath, it is you that I would will to live.

For me you have been sensational, love at its finest, I need to tell the world how you give.

I watch you as the Sun rise across your brow, till the moon finally glows in its place.

Thank you God, for blessing me with her, even more for helping me understand your grace.

There were times that I wanted to give in and give up, on the race of how to cope.

Nevertheless, you cheered me on, ran side by side through tribulations, you gave me hope.

I still remember the days of feeling lost and alone as the faith within started to dwindle.

You and that heave ho attitude is what kept me going and the love you added for kindle.

I still smell a bouquet of my favorite fragrances when I even entertain the thought of you.

If you were an invention, you would be "light" for the brightness you emit in all that you do.

I love telling the world about you, while watching our flag, honoring our love being raised.

I forever place you on a pedestal, next to thrones in our empire, lifting your name in praise.

I would climb the highest mountains backwards and backstroke all the way non-stop.

Just to see you the conqueror, you my queen, just to see you reach the top.

I am truly glad God made only one of you; two would be more than a soul could bear.

Even though you are only one, there are days you are difficult to have to share.

So I'll continue to hide my enviousness, of how much I value your being and time.

Remembering you as your sensational self, for every reason and every rhyme.

You Are My Everything...

I was looking for real love, and you pulled it out of thin air.

I needed someone who truly understood me, and you were there.

I wanted to caress someone, who knew the meaning of close and dear.

I never imagined I'd see your love in everything around me, you are always near.

I play it forward, and think of the moments to come that I don't have to share you.

I never had a love to call my own, so yes when it comes to you; I have a selfish view.

I quietly retain my thoughts on how you can do no wrong, but you'll never know.

I think you are so beautiful, that in my mind your shine will never turn to a glow.

I tell everyone about you, proud to be your man, your knight in shining armor.

I love to see you laugh, but I like better being your personal prince charmer.

I wish I knew magic, when I open my hand to you a bouquet of flowers would appear.

I would then take you to a far away secluded place like love's ionosphere.

I could re-invent Valentine's Day to be special each and everyday of the week.

I will make music with timeless rhythm, heartbeats to love, if that is what you seek.

I keep thinking of new things we can share, hoping to never awake from this dream.

I wonder if you go on without me, how life with coffee would be with no cream.

I know in you, I have found my best friend flowing freely from love's stream.

I just want to keep you happy, as you have done for me, you are my everything.

"Simply, splendidly, soft..."

I thought it was her attire that she wears,

Or the conditioner that she uses on her hair.

Maybe it was the lotions or creams she love so much

that gave her that radiant and silky touch.

Suddenly, I found myself within her cozy loft.

It was as if I was in a dream that was simply,
splendidly, soft.

Can't quite make the visuals, is she Oriental or Asian,

filled with glowing soul inside?

Is she Spanish or Caucasian with brown skin?

She walks like a sister, oh what a ride.

I just know I found myself in her loft.

She will never be forgotten, she is

Simply, splendidly, soft.

I Wonder…

I wonder what God was thinking of…

When he decided to give earth, one from above.

With the beauty she has within the stare of her eyes,

I am weaken, yet strengthen, love has no disguise.

I wonder what God had on his mind…

Giving her a silken touch with sensual body designs.

I once saw her in a dream, can dreams prevail?

I am one with her, the closeness, when she exhales, I inhale.

I wonder if God, will one day let me see his master-plan…

On living life on life's terms, how he preserved this woman for this man.

God created imaginations, I wonder if he planned for me to go afar-

I'm imagining her, the Goddess of Love, and me…the Love Czar.

I wonder if she knows how I feel about her. I want to be her protector…

Comforting her every moment, my mission – never neglect her!

Can you feel it? It's growing moment by moment ceasing to rest, gaining momentum as I lay my head on her breast.

This is it…will the both of us conceive –

WE ARE ONE …Only if we both believe!

ENERGY...

I lay tossing and turning, just can't find that peace of mind.

My thoughts running together, it seems so hard to unwind.

I watched you sleeping so peaceful, so relaxed, looking oh so tender.

I want you to have the best life has to offer in me, my one true, agenda.

As I move about through the night, back and forth trying not to be heard;

Not wanting you to notice my unrest, you offer those encouraging words...

Endearing and comforting you say "are you ok...is there something wrong?

It is that moment I feel your energy, I regain the strength, and again I'm strong.

I need you to know your power, when I even hear the sound of your voice.

When my ideas back into a corner, I'm reminded of the knowledge of choice.

I'm thankful for you and the energy that you give every time we caress.

Today, because of you...I feel alive, vibrant, motivated, and I'm impressed.

I have many ideas; I need you to stay grounded when I'm feeling my flow,

I need your opinions, with mine alone, I feel dressed up with no where to go.

My hope is that our love for one another never loses its luster or gleam.

That our touch maintains its sincerity, and reality finds its way thru our

DREAMS!!!

MEMORIES

Has the time come for us to look at the things that really matters most.

Walking along the beach, visiting family and friends from coast to coast?

Remember going to the zoo, the animals, seeing how they live and breed.

Or the walks through nature's path and attending to her special needs.

I can still remember going to a neighbor's home and lending a helping hand.

Going to church, listening to the choir sing, thinking "oh, isn't life grand!"

America! I say thank you, for all the freedom and life you have given.

With all of your wondrous beauty, there is <u>no</u> <u>land,</u> <u>nowhere</u> worth living.

We've come to enjoy the American way of life, dream of dreams come true.

Many races, over a billion faces, live in this land through and through.

Although, all not related, an invisible thread has sown us all together.

As we have learned in love or in tragedy we intertwine no matter the weather.

So let's continue our evening walks with the one's we love and cherish.

In our downtowns or along the beaches and let not our freedoms perish.

I still have some kind words to say, love to share, and so much yet to learn.

For me, as life brings forth a new day, it's new life that I seem to yearn.

I, yet look to the sky as my limit, and a challenge to be better or at my best.

To give back that which was freely given to me before I am laid to rest.

Only You...

Can fill my world with joy.

Remembrance of love as a boy;

I love you... Do you love me?

____yes   ____no

Freedom to love... Freedom to be...

The untainted feeling that dared to rise,

to soar across our nation skies.

Love has never eluded anyone.

The recipe for life, that simmers to perfection-

Yet it is never done.

As life grows on, LOVE its twin from the start

Nancy, you and I share them both, never will the twain part.

As a child love was mystical, to a man endearing and robust.

Sincere, dedicated, caring, responsible, so with you my heart I'll trust!

On my behalf I'll cherish you, for each moment your love I'll earn.

Till you're finally convinced our love is a cinch, tried by fire yet burns, in the hearts of many, but only a plenty receives of the lessons love learns.

Love doesn't love anyone; it's the individual(s) who is in need of giving.

The one, who knows not LOVE, soon learns that life is not worth living!

So I'll caress you all day long, even if at times, just in thought.

You my dove, keep my focus on LOVE, it can never be sold or bought.

You are my fantasy in reality, my sincere dream come true.

Our LOVE will not only conquer Valentines, it will soar to heights anew!

"The Way You Do That Thing You Do..."

It seems mystical, how I can be astounded by just the look of you.

Something has changed since we first met, "ah a more radiant view!"

I still look in your eyes and find comfort during my moments of pain.

Never, have I longed for another's touch, or will, during your reign.

When we caress you embrace my body, yet, you capture my pulsating heart.

I feel like the hunter, that's been captured by his game from the start!

From the first time the canal filled, the boat sailed its way up river.

The sensation is still the same, I still break sweat and my body still quiver.

You are so amazing! I thought once "It's just a mind set!" That wasn't true.

No, there is something special about the way you do the things you do!

We traveled across country, while making our marks in the clouds,

I watched you strut down the aisle as your charisma spoke out loud.

It's the innocence you exude even though you're not; it's the ultimate intrigue.

To know that your high society, filled with class, set in the "AAA" league.

All the reasons I want to give you the best, over and over times again.

Who should be so fortunate, to have a lover and best friend – all in one man?

My search for you has long been over from the first moment we met.

As I will continue to serenade you with love, my words you'll not forget.

For I will uphold all of my vows whether silently or outspoken,

This ménage built with love, trust and honesty will never be broken.

Daily, I thank God for letting our paths cross and our hearts intertwine.

Only he knew, with me love was not only a mystery, but clandestine.

So, I shout to the world and galaxies of old and new,

"No one does it better, when you do that thing you do!"

Concerts by the Sea

Four days ago, it was just a plan.

A thought, a getaway, a woman and her man.

Too much work along with life placed a wedge.

So some time in Hawaii was their pledge.

She had planned it all, which had his mind spinning.

For she knew this would be ideal for yet another beginning.

It seemed mystical the loudness of the quiet sun.

The radiance and brilliance it gave her smile until each day was done.

The chatter and laughter once more filled the air.

While thoughts transcended on one another like no moments to spare.

Simply amazing no sirens, alarms, just waves washing ashore.

Crashing against the rocks, like musicians repeating a score.

Something good happens in everyone's life that cannot be put into words.

You are that for me, in my life you encompass all the verbs.

You are the action that motivates me, even during the times you let me be.

Of all the joyous noises that nature brings, and life's unwavering fee, my life would be nothing without you. For you are my concerts by the sea!

SOMETIMES...

Sometimes, when I look into your eyes,
I wonder if you realize the depths that I see.

I look pass your beauty and your loving stare.
Deep into your soul, sifting through emotions
to the heart that rests in there.

At first glance I see the pounding of sincerity.
The steady flow of kindness, finally whispers of
"He loves me, He loves me not, and He loves me!"

Simply because memories are not inconsistent unless
The mind allows them to be...
"Yes! He loves me!"

Sometimes, when I hear your voice
something inside me gets excited,
my bubble of joy casually explodes.

I hear your voice in distant winds.
Consistent words to guide me,
through my trials and life's overloads.

I hear the tone when you taught me to
Learn how to agree to disagree.

Because I may be right that instant, nevertheless
Winning is not always suitable for me.

So I will forever hear you whether in
conversation or in song.

For your wisdom is God sent and
you've never steered me wrong.

Sometimes, when I needed the assurance of touch,
I wonder when I place the order why can't we go
Dutch?

THE END...

When it's the end there is no compromise.

Vision is blinded and truth is disguised.

Everyone is right; somebody needs to wrong.

Who'll sing the beginning verse of this "It's The End" song?

Has time carried us or has it been just a matter of time?

It's always over something small, simply no reason or rhyme.

Is there not anything worth salvaging from our gains?

Or will we add more misery to our pains?

Awakening not in view of the other's lair,

or captivating the scent of the other's hair.

Can we accept not hearing that famous "I love you..." upon waking up?

Or being there to catch one's feelings when things go abrupt.

Can we do without the laughter in the middle of the night?

Can we go on existing knowing someone else is holding the other tight?

After looking back on things and giving it an ample review; maybe it's not the end I want, but a momentary lapse of remembering how much

"I do love you!"

Here We Go Again!

I thought love had its limitations;

Except within the confines of my imaginations.

It seems we are withstanding the test of times.

Good, bad, indifferent, without rhythm or rhyme.

I can still remember the first time you said

"I love you" to me.

Just as I remember the first calming of my troubled sea.

The sea of love.

I've tread those waters for so many years.

Only looking for lost treasures, but finding tears.

You came into my life, and let me into yours-

We will rewrite the love songs with unheard scores.

Just like our first touch we will forever blend,

So hold on tight because here we go again.

Desire'

She seemed to have come to me in a dream, as I reach to touch her in thought.

I know her, and have known her, can't shake this feeling; mystically I'm caught.

It is not just an attraction; magnetically I'm drawn by her beauty and her zeal.

Miles away I hear her voice in a whisper, I need her near, by wind, I send my appeal.

I see her in all the wonders that surround me; I can find her love in a breath of air.

Inside the flow of a gentle breezes onboard a yacht destination anywhere.

I detect her being from the sun when I need energy, and her comfort from the moon.

She is the desire of desires; I hear her music, learn of her lyrics, and dance with her tune.

Through telepathy she spoke to me, as if to ease my spirit and remove any doubt.

Suddenly, there was no need to speak, through her eyes I knew what this was about.

She makes it easy to be of love, in love, about love, endless moments of pleasure.

Your desires are being served, cast time from the menu; true happiness has no measure.

I have tropical dreams, and island fantasies; anytime she enters or prances near my lair.

A rainbow or the largest box of crayons, could not describe her inner beauty or compare.

A dream was now reality, I remembered her from not long ago, to many coincidences.

The soft skin, the radiant smile, the smell of her hair in the shower after it rinses.

The silken touch as she stroked my brow, and that walk as she passes, how her hips sway;

No one could have told me I would encounter her again this way.

She was just a dream when I was a child, but somehow she came back for more.

I realize today she is not just one woman; she represents women, from times before.

Amazingly, you can learn a lot from a dream, especially if you are blessed to awaken,

And remember the things you valued most before your dream was taken.

"BEAUTIFUL"

The wind in a soul,

Life big and bold.

God's endearment through creation,

a voice of gold.

A Sister's Sister.

A Brother's Sister.

Hey! Have you heard her Mister?

She implies wisdom from within and lets it flow,

As words pass her lips the syllables glow.

She reminds me of ol' G, Black Women

Young, old, all the Mammies;

She'll receive the original Black Grammy.

We've been blessed to have the Roberta Flacks'

At our backs, the Erika Badu's to carry us through.

However, today we are FREE...

We are blessed with an "India Arie!"

02.14.07

I want to cry,

But the pain over-shadows my tears…

So I write,

I write but the words cannot equal

Or

Describe my inner desires.

ODE FROM A POET...TO A READER!

I'm sitting here trying to ponder the outcome,

Where we're headed and then some.

Who's taking over, what's taking over, we did call 'em wars, now they're conflicts.

News is no longer news it's abused; it's all about killing and comments by Dixie Chicks.

Rappers come and go like Coolio.

Artists don't just die in the streets; it's gone to the studio.

What some won't do to get a dollar, would you take nine slugs to the body like Fifty Cent?

Just to join up with Dr. Dre and Eminem to make a mint.

That may be a dream, but my reality is that I owe our uncle thirty-seven g's.

So when I excuse myself and tell you I don't have time to kick it, back up homie please!

The only thing I got time to do is to sit here and try to put words to paper,

to tell the untold story of my life, to capitalize on some loot, and bring an end to this caper.

You see my life to most would seem like something out of a dream, truth be told.

However, when it's all out in print, and your loot is spent, my story will be like gold.

Not the gold that is spent or the gold that you rent, but spoken gold, golden words.

Words to live by, words to survive by, gold nouns, pronouns, adjectives and verbs.

Take my words mince them, mix them, but you can't take my experience out of them.

My words will be your new keys to the song of life hymn.

The hymn that you'll hum, when things go dark hymn.

The hymn that you'll hum, when you need a spark hymn.

The hymn that you'll sing in your heart hymn.

The hymn you'll learn to recite hymn, when trouble begins to depart hymn.

I write to give you strength, I write to give you the power.

The power that emulates from love, peace and hope in the seconds that make the hour.

SO THE NEXT TIME YOU WANT A GOOD READ, AND YOU GO TO BUY A BOOK,

TRY TO FIND THIS AUTHOR, ON THE SHELVES THE OTHER AUTHORS SHOOK!

BLIND

To be blind is not only, not having vision;

For it is more intense to be blinded by self-denial.

"On The Inside"

Some people let the exterior lead them through a maze within life's trials.

While others just follow behind accepting mere designs of life's denials.

How can the hand be quicker than the eye, if realism is right in your face?

Doctrines, laws, justice, institutions, and amendments to the same, are they being erased?

Something seems unclear to me, we talk of justice and peace, but that's not what we promote.

We talk of equality, in rights, real estate, business, education, and we talk of ONE VOTE.

Truth be told, I could die today for my honesty, found in a place with a slit throat.

Simply because America and the Americans would rather live and die in DENIAL.

No one is willing to stand for truth even if it was stacked neatly in a pile.

I heard someone say "I don't mind dying; just give me something to die for!"

There may be many things, but tell me why "Truth" did not rate high or even score?

As I grew from childhood into manhood, I was told the truth would set you free.

Today truth will have me in a cell fighting for life or dangling on a rope tied to a tree.

Slavery today is high tech, nothing has changed, and the South just came to the North.

I've even learned to smile when in pain, to never let 'em see you sweat and so forth.

I have accepted the trials but not my fate; I can be handicapped but refuse to be broken.

I am a man first; Black second and nevertheless I will never be a token.

I will not be hoodwinked or bamboozled; I have the mental capabilities to survive.

You see I learned from what you taught; I can go into the wilderness and stay alive.

Because soon and very soon even money will be of no value to you or me.

We all are going to have to meet our Maker and enter our final plea.

I'm glad there is a God of mercy, because it is his mercy that we'll need on this ride,

And lest we all forget, we will not be judged outwardly, but for what is on the Inside.

Writings on the wall...

What is it? What does it mean? All of these writings on the walls.

Scribbling, jargon, minced words, graffiti written in the halls.

On the side of boxcars, buildings, alleyways, some with colorful designs.

Is it an expression of art, or just some gang member out of his mind?

Some might say it's the challenge, of working on someone's last nerves,

While others think, "it's my voice, I write…" I can get the attention I deserve.

Let me think; we're talking about people, who would spend their last dime on paint,

Their only desire a smooth surface to write, sentences that start with "I ain't!"

Now I pose the challenge…who would help them if they could?

To find meaning to a measure of rule, to really beautify the hood!

I'm willing to wager, with little direction, we could find positive features in them,

like they did in New York, someone took the time and taught a spiritual hymn.

The past and present has taught that bickering and resistance only pulls us apart.

Let's find common ground to pull another up, a handshake…a good way to start!

How about this…I share the best part of me with you; I expect nothing in return.

You see, one thing I know is true, GIVING is a lesson well learned.

If I want you to be at your best, then just maybe, I should be at mine.

So let's take your talent, add a little twist, change it to an architectural design!!!

"Where have all the children gone?"

The Sun was out and the sky was clear as I passed by a city park today,

But where have the children gone, the grounds are barren no one out at play.

The swings just hung, not one child sliding down the

Slides, running or climbing the monkey bars.

Not one little kid running so fast to have fun, while reaching for the stars.

I remember those days, "Hey where's the Sand Box?" I asked one man.

He replied, "Filled with cement! A politician gave a speech, and needed somewhere to stand!"

I still wondered where the kids are. I sat in the swing and began to glide.

When my eyes closed the passing breeze sent illusions of our nation's countryside.

All I could vision was time moving fast, kids were running and crying,

I heard gunshots, rapid fire, and then I saw a group of kids just dying.

One threw up a gang sign and shouted "What's up cuz, are you Folks!"

But you couldn't see his eyes to see his soul; they were hidden by his lolk's.

You know his sunglasses, his Ray Charles' that's what ol' gees wear!

So you can't see their eyes, if they look at you with the murderous stare.

It started in one city now it's local; kids don't stand a chance,

If they don't claim something, they'll die for nothing, forget about the romance.

Is there any wonder where the kid's have gone, ain't no love in the room!

They're taught money is the bride, and flat out Sin is the groom.

Somewhere, some way things are going to have to change,

Parents must be parents again, instead their acting deranged.

As I opened my eyes the breeze subsides the swing began to stop,

I thought of all the things that I could do, to help a kid reach the top.

I could be a better living example, by being the best that I can be.

So that when a kid needs someone to look to, I may be who they see.

"IF ONLY YOU BELIEVE..."

If only you believe that even in your darkest moment or hour, when situations become overwhelming and your strength seems to loose it's power.

It feels as though you've misplaced the responsibility of being accountable.

As you look for a friend to talk to, someone with love insurmountable.

I cry out, "My life is good." I encompass love, I am love, and I sow love's seed.

Yet I feel hollow, I am thirsty for being complete; it's God that I need.

I yearn to do all the good I have imagined, as my cup seems to overflow.

A sincere handshake, a warm hug, a tender kiss as I

I pray to maintain a tender ear, for another soul to find solace and confide.

To promote peace, the innermost part of my heart; never letting compassion subside.

I pledge to be a soldier in heaven's army, regardless of life's many trials and pain.

I leave this legacy while passing through this life; my living has not been in vain.

"MIRACLES"

Miracle (mir'a kal) to wonder at – an event or action that apparently contradicts known scientific laws and is hence thought to be due to supernatural causes, esp. to an act of God.

Where did they come from? Did they really happen? Am I a puppet in someone's dream?

As far back as I can remember, I can recall events and situations ending not as they seem.

I remember being in life changing times, my mind so clouded I had no vision, I couldn't see.

My road was filled with loose gravel, when I heard a still voice say "Have a little faith in me!"

I still had my doubts, because I heard a voice and saw no one; I'd better check my mental state.

Plus nothing of substance never cross my path and disaster always seem to seal my fate.

However, through it all I still felt a sense of comfort, an encompassing spirit of love.

Then you said you would never leave me or forsake me, a covenant from heaven above.

Now when I sit back and reminisce on the those times when I felt the pendulum sway,

when I wanted to give in to the darkness, you placed Angels all along my way.

I've learned over the years that Angels can appear in many forms and different ways.

Just like you I can see them in others young and old, tattered or torn and different displays.

There were times I've often wondered why my life was blessed and in so many ways spared.

Why I received mercy and leniency as I search the good of others lives I've compared?

Oh, I've done a lot of good, but I recall begging to die before the war of good and evil was won.

I thought I couldn't go on, life's struggles to tough, but today I know my job here is not done.

I need to share the miracles, the blessings, the love, and all the wonders that have befallen me.

The only thing that comes to a sleeper is a dream, today the vision is clear and I see.

I no longer entertain or ponder negative thoughts, and struggles are hidden on a shelf;

I will never again wonder about miracles if it happens, because my miracle has been life itself.

When I lay myself down for rest, and after a period of time, I'm allowed to open my eyes.

The blessing of the breath of life gives me strength to endure life's heavy sighs.

If I am given the strength, to stand and walk to place, one foot in front of the next.

I can pass through life's trials, tribulations, and mysteries no matter how complex.

I've learned to watch my tongue, to beware of others feelings, and not to speak in haste.

To give thanks for fulfilling my palate with nourishment and the substance I can taste.

After experiencing it, I could never imagine what it would be like to be unable to hear,

All the joyous noises in the world, good noises, bad noises, even the noises of fear.

Today, there is one sense that I personally place on a pedestal high above much,

It gives me more pleasure than any physical attribute and that's the miracle of touch.

Have you ever noticed the difference after a rain or after the first fall of snow, can you tell?

It's intense, a force of energy, it has vigor; it's the miracle of being able to smell.

So when you look upon your life for miracles, keep in mind it's not the size that count,

MIRACLES come in different sizes, shapes, and forms, but a MIRACLE is a MIRACLE in any amount!

"TIME"

The noise I hear is the ringing of <u>Time.</u>

Heartbeats, rhythms of breath, are they mimic or mime?

Is life supposed to be repetitious because I keep waking up?

To realities that stagnate me instead of growth, and runneth over my cup.

<u>Time</u> is no longer my friend cause under pressure it runs out, over and out.

Through <u>Time</u> comes many questions, yet after <u>Time</u> very little doubt.

We all try to stay within frames of <u>Time</u>.

Click, click goes the camera of life, is your life cola, orange, grape, code red, or lemon-lime.

Click, click goes the camera of life, your camera...is it set on bright or dim?

I lay wounded; <u>Time</u> says that my chances are slim.

Too much <u>Time</u> has festered in this open sore.

Now, I'm infected by <u>Time</u>, infected to the core.

I must admit, I never respected <u>Time</u> for a second.

So this day was to come, this my day of reckon.

<u>Time</u> is not my judge; <u>Time</u> is the prosecutor of life's law.

<u>Time</u> bares no blame, and life's not the luck of the draw.

Time can be life's best accessory with God on your side.

Faith is all you need to breathe each breath with pride.

I once was told "the body was fearfully and wonderfully made; with enough Time it'll heal itself."

If you want the knowledge the good book contains, dust off the Bible on your shelf.

Sometimes, I wonder how I got through many situations some days.

Why God still loves me, after I done my will in so many different ways.

The noise I hear is the ringing of Time.

Heartbeats, rhythms of breath are they mimic or mime?

I realize now my Time is short, to say how short I'd be guessing.

But not to short to realize that God loves me, and that is my ultimate Blessing.

"...And The Chariot Swung Low!"

The night's moon had disappeared, and the morning sun was already shinning.

Another promising day for life, as we had no idea of redesigning,

what we sometimes take for granted, the sound of voices, the visuals, and even one's touch;

how did I come to this space, it's overwhelming and sudden… "I miss you so much!"

I just talked to you, I held your hand, we hugged, and then I saw you walk away.

Then far off in the distance, I began to realize your pain; a quiet voice whispered "Just Pray."

Something devastating has happened; our peace has been torn from its core.

I along with countless others, hope you rest in God, for me you rest no more.

I often think can we go on? There's too much pain, grief, and sorrow to share.

I just keep reminding others and myself…God said, "I'll not give you what you can't bear."

It seems as though, our lives of dreams went up in smoke, as debris fell from high above.

But what really fell, as all pulled together, three things God left us, Faith, Hope, and Love.

Thank you God, for carrying us, and blessing us,
because sometimes we know not good,

Man's mistake is following his own will, and not
following your will, as we should.

Again, terror and the terrorists have shook the sleeping
giant, as evil pace, then roam;

and the chariot swung low, God embracing them all,
took them to Heaven's home.

"TIMES OF THE SIGN"

So many years have come and gone, as we grow with new relations;

We never cease searching for the truth, even though we set our limitations.

For truth is love, at its highest level of esteem, permeating many stimulations;

Yet the truth as we know it, finds it hard to be the cure all, in many situations.

If the truth will set you free, then why is it for many just another's ideations?

Count the times you've heard "Just tell me the truth…" in the tone of provocation.

Why ask for the truth, and at the same time pain, if you won't accept realization?

Live a lie for too long, and then the truth becomes blinding chapters of revelations.

Life reveals, the truth cannot be colored or shaded because of its adoration.

Honesty somehow perseveres when truth may seem to go on vacation.

Hopefully, through love we can grow in truth and not on just simulations,

As we speak words of truth, live the principles of truth, less the accusations.

We as a people, a family, need not fake the truth, just to reap the indignations.

That follows dishonesty, consents to deceit, and destruction with its ramifications.

Let us all do an about-face on injustice, as we awaken from this hallucination.

That we are so mighty and indestructible, and give God back his Glorification!

When They Write About Me..

I wonder if anyone will realize how much and how hard I loved you.

If someone will remember how special you made my world as I passed through.

Maybe someone will think of the songs that I've carried for you in my heart.

Songs of love, words of praise, and some songs I couldn't begin to start.

It would have meant to surrender to the fact that I wouldn't want to live one day without you by my side.

I could be in Chicago and you in Paris, yet nothing could separate our hearts in glide.

When they write about me, will there be one to testify that I never sought another soul to take your place?

How when I met you it was not in haste, can anyone identify with knowing the end of a life long chase?

So what is love? To know love is to have loved, only to give love, only to live love, so I love the world; but you more than anything in it.

When they write about me, will anyone be able to distinguish how I look into your eyes and see your heart?

How I know your pain and your gentle side, for you not be loving and kind tears you apart.

Will there be one that could narrate the depths of my inner soul, about how it's not about me, but really all about you.

Will there be some to write how even when I see you in the distant sun or the mediocre moonlight, I am positive it's you.

Simply because I can feel you, I know your touch before the sensation of contact, your warmth before penetration of my sphere.

I know the taste of your brow, even the water in your eyes before you shed a tear.

So when they write about me, the one thing that will forever be true,

is that they won't be writing about one, because if they write about me they will be writing about you. Because you are me and I am you.

When they write about me, whether the words are many or even a few, I want the world to know that there is no me without you.

WHEN IT'S ALL OVER!!!

Daybreak, it's still pretty quiet, very few are on the move.

Some are carrying on from last night, others trying to find a new groove.

My reality seems like a dream, it's mid June, but I'm a December baby-

Should I be cold or just cold during the heat, most times my world is hazy.

I still find it hard to decipher when to love, how to love, or if love should even be, entered into my mode, not part of the street code, love will find it hard to love me.

You see to understand, you need to live my walk, start with Chicago's Westside.

Gangs are king, young gangsters dream, breakfast served up with a homicide.

Pimps, players, whores and prostitutes, show youngsters how to ghetto survive.

They push dope, they push there is no hope, unless it's a Benz that you drive.

Deep in minds of many, to get what is good or plenty, knowledge of the game a must.

Application of the game determines you share of the green "In God We Trust."

It's a sin and a shame, in the hood the color is green; keeps most folks color blind.

What I wouldn't do for some loot, things so tough, can't get enough, I'll sell a baby that's not mine.

Society has taught me that nothing else matters, so I have to do what I gotta do!

I can't see no way out, so I lie, I have no pride…what?" I'll steal the "J" out of Jew.

You look at me as though I'm the problem, but all of you made me all I am today.

You taught me, it's a dog eat dog world; I'll kill my brother if he gets in my way.

You don't want to hear the truth, so you showed me how to live in denial.

Denying that I have feelings, to rise from this ghetto life of trials.

I only realized just a moment ago, that it's not me but my expressions that you fear.

When I sing, you think I'm angry; you're amazed when I cry and don't shed a tear.

We may differ outwardly; however, in our hearts we have the same agenda.

To find peace amongst each other, although, the first thing to learn is how to surrender.

Someone was killed in a drive-by today, someone's son or daughter taken away.

The family will be told, how the events unfold, what part in the funeral they'll play.

The resentments will be strong, but God will show you how to tarry along.

This day will be a new beginning, the lyrics to a save your own life song.

"Yesterday's Tomorrow"

I promised a real good friend a favor the other day.

As fate would have it I got busy and the promise went astray.

I thought, as always my friend should understand my toils and strife.

All the changes I go through, less I forget this friend gave me life.

I did not recall how over time, I've made many promises with tears.

How He carries through day to day, and how it's lasted for years.

Today, I've noticed the impact it has on the people I love so much.

I see the pain in their eyes, when I don't realize the hearts I touch.

Today, I will make a difference when I speak on spoken words.

Such as the promises I've made to myself and the ones others heard.

My right now moments means the world; I will not wallow in sorrow.

I know He who holds the truth, also holds my Yesterday's tomorrow.

You see if you take time to think; Yesterday's tomorrow is today!

Challenge yourself get busy NOW, and don't promise your life away.

JUST IN CASE...

When the day begins with a shaky beginning, as my spirit is dimmed by the light:

I look to the umbrella for my soul as the sun in my life begins to lose it height.

I want to retain the fond memories, all the dreams, and the treasured aspirations of my plight.

Remembering how time after time you gave me visions during the moments I had no sight.

I just want to live my life spiritually, patterned after the God I behold.

Because if it is true as I believe, I'll be in that number to tread the streets of gold.

All my life I've prayed to God, not seeing or touching him, but by faith I am sustained.

I am convinced that he lives; I see his footprints in the sand, miracles no others attained.

Miracles in my life alone and I am just an individual, whose life was so complex;

Riddled with mysteries and miseries, it's amazing that I can think one moment to the next.

My life: A modern day gangster? A drug czar? A gentleman of leisure? You fill in the blanks!

I recall wanting to commit suicide to prevent homicide on Lake Michigan and Pacific Ocean banks.

I wanted to be a man, I thought I was a man; could I just be a father like my dad had been?

I know the answer today is constant prayer and giving my will to God, and live not with sin.

I have no clue what tomorrow will bring and I can't change yesterday, all I have is now.

I want to love without worrying about being loved and let it cultivate like a farmer with a plow.

I have no idea when the curtains of my life will be drawn; I just want to run an honest race,

so when those clouds burst open, the face of God is revealed, I want to be ready JUST IN CASE,,,

To my mother, Ruby L. Eddings with love.

The first thing I would like you to know is how much I love YOU.

How much of a joy it has been to be a part of YOU.

The kindness that I have in my heart today is because of YOU.

Letting go and letting God, is an attribute that I noticed from YOU.

To support another's ideas even if it were not popular was… YOU,

life is for the living, doing God's work includes forgiving that's YOU.

You are more than a mother, you are a confidant, people confide in YOU.

You have many talents, you have vision, and an unwavering love in YOU.

A gentle soul, with a gentle touch, is what I experienced with YOU. You persevere, when others tried to antagonize, you walk with God inside YOU.

It's amazing how things you taught came to pass; I look for knowledge in YOU.

I truly thank you for the standards, principles and morals I've gain from YOU.

God's using you as a beacon of light; he lets his Holy Spirit shine through YOU.

Thanks for being my mother, my friend, my everything.

Your son,   Melvin Eddings

"My Mother..."

Some say a mother's work is never done.

Even though you do it with ease and a little fun.

A mother's love gives me a clearer view on

How to love, and know God's love. If it weren't for you...

I could never give back all you've given;

However, I can reflect God's love in my living.

Thank you, for all you done and may do,

You're too awesome...if it weren't for you.

"I Testify…"

Along with your mother's wit and wisdom you raised
me.

Even today as we see eye to eye, you still amaze me.

It is surreal to understand

How God created mothers…

How he knew the winning combinations

Of bonding, love, trust and the ground it covers.

How nurturing, faith and only

A mother's words or touch

Would span throughout millenniums.

Nothing I can think of matters as much.

So go ahead enjoy this day…

And every other that you breathe.

You are God's best creation

And this I truly believe.

THANKSGIVING

Once upon a time long ago, someone was inspired to set a day aside to reflect,

All the blessings that had come their way, by God through another with respect.

Before we matured we called it luck; today we know blessings come in many forms.

Maybe through family or a loved one, that God guides us to the light after the storms.

It's the time we gather to show love, so in tradition I'd like to take the time to recall,

To write about my blessings, feelings of love, and the things that matter to me most of all.

Thanks for giving me the most important part of you.

Thanks for giving me a renewed and fresh spirited view.

Thanks for giving me the warm kisses in my time of need.

Thanks for giving me new ideas to keep me up to speed.

Thanks for giving me provisions of soup on days I am not well.

Thanks for giving me your honest appraisal when others will not tell.

Thanks for giving me a hug; there are times when I feel so alone.

Thanks for giving me warmth under the covers when I'm chilled to the bone.

Thanks for giving me friendship and showing me how to care.

Thanks for giving me your version of indifference on how to love is to share.

Thanks for giving me your undivided attention when I look into your eyes.

Thanks for giving me the notion that I can reach the stars in your skies.

Thanks for giving me your most important piece of real estate – your heart.

Thanks for giving me the strength to believe that nothing could keep us apart.

Thanks for giving me a new lease on this dream we call life.

Thanks for giving me the gift God set aside long ago, you as my wife.

So I say hip, hip, hooray, for the blessings and all the treasures they give,

To longevity in love as long as we both shall live.

"Sister Harvey"

What makes a person special, are the things that they stand for.

Here is a breakdown of what "S.i.s. H.a.r.v.e.y" means to me.

S= stands for her spiritual nature that only God can measure.

I= stands for her inspiring wisdom that has given many the gift of pleasure.

S= stands again for her sincerity in showing us how God loved, as we should love as such.

H= stands for healing hands, helping hands, praying hands with a devoted touch.

A= stands for angelic, God had to leave some angels here in his place.

R= stands for rhythm, as a teacher you must be constant to keep a steady pace.

V= stands for vital vigor, to live to see 100 years you must show up ready everyday…

E= stands for eternal standards, can you imagine learning 36,500 ways to pray.

Y= stands for the yearning to understand rather than be understood,

To live right, to live healthy, and to give a hundred years of good.

So to you, Sis. Harvey, I wish you all the best that his life has to offer.

Have a wonderful and blessed, Happy Birthday!

WHAT A GIFT...

I want to tell you a short story,

Of a woman who is filled with glory.

As you listen, lift your heart to pray,

To wish our Sis. Harvey, a Happy Birthday.

Here is a person of many feats.

A student, a scholar, a teacher complete,

Who made education special and learning a treat.

And then there's that mother's wit to guide you along,

That made you stand tall, appears wise and strong.

A mother's mother, a father's mother, a
brother/sister's mother;

When it comes to nurturing there is no other,

That can make you feel like you are one of her own,

Leading and teaching many through childhood till
grown.

God came into her life, and filled it with hopes then
joy,

As he then showed her how through him longevity
would employ.

So he allowed her to see years, one through one
hundred and more,

Many jewels, dreams that came true, as he tallied the
score.

He gave her all of her heart's desire, even some she
never asked for.

However, there is one gift, that she will ever be indebted to share,

And that was the breath of life and one hundred years to care.

She has remain ever so grateful, lifting his name in every way,

Looking for her final blessing, her name called on judgment day.

Until then I've noticed her, how she will spiritually roam,

Up to the great day God calls her to her heavenly home.

HAPPY BIRTHDAY!

Sis. Harvey, with love!

"A MINUTE IN TIME"

Tender as the day is long,

It is your touch that makes me strong.

Just the thought of you; and my heart begins to soar,

To the beat, the rhythm of an unwritten music score.

I'm missing you, I'm needing you, I've got you on my mind.

I need you in my life all day, right now; for just a minute in time.

I love the way you sing my name.

In my confusion you want to take the blame.

You are the reason I take responsibility,

During the season of my accountability.

With you by my side I face very little strife.

Your love is in season and the reason for my life.

I'm missing you, I'm needing you, I've got you on my mind.

I need you in my life all day, right now; for just a minute in time.

To have you, to hold you-

To kiss you, because I miss you.

I'm missing you, I'm needing you, I've got you on my mind.

I need you in my life all day, right now; for just a minute in time.

"A Beacon of Light"

On this day that man has set aside to show great love for you,

Cherishing moments past and present about the great job you do.

Some thank you for being a good mother and raising the kids.

While other's thank you for support and standing by them like you did.

I stopped to wonder how many of us lose our vision and finally our sight.

Only to realize the vision we search for was inside of you "A beacon of light."

That's what you are to me, my way when I'm lost, with my mind gone astray.

I can always count on you in a whisper, "son get on your knees and pray."

Let God be whom you look to, for no man has a better idea or plan.

The God of Abraham, Isaac and Jacob, on his rock you can stand.

Only a mother lead by the Holy Spirit can give that kind of advice.

So thank you mother for raising me with love and teaching me Jesus is Christ.

I also want to thank you for all you've done and more, today heavens in sight.

Most of all, I thank you for your guidance because you are my beacon of light.

I Call your Name

1st verse

When I wake up early in the morning and
 The sunshine warms my face.
Everything seems mystical, my thoughts travel
From place to place.
I'll gather all my tools and armor that I'll
Need on my way.
While thanking you Lord for all that you've done
And your blessing me another day.

Chorus

So whether I drop down on my knees or pause
For silent prayer,
Thank you Lord for always being there.
I may falter but your love stays the same.
So I cry out Lord! Lord! I call your name.

2nd verse

While on my daily journey trouble seems to find my path.

Life seems to be a struggle as I wrestle Satan's wrath.

So many times I've wanted to give up and plainly say I just don't care.

And get on board with Lucifer my soul to be the fare.

But it's then I feel your messenger with wings spread out wide.

Telling me how you love me, and why your son had died.

He said every time you're feeling low and you seem all alone.

Dial God's number, he's always up and never has a busy phone.

Chorus

So whether I drop down on my knees or pause for silent prayer.

Thank you Lord for always being there.

I may falter, but your love stays the same

So I cry out Lord! Lord! I call your name.

ALWAYS

Always stay the course in your faith of your hopes…

And never expect anyone

To follow as you lead to lift your dreams

And aspirations.

Melvin Eddings